In this stunning new book, Canisia Lubrin brings her signature epic vision to a radiant elegy for her mother. Its axis of astonishment belongs as much to history as to today—interwoven and unresolvable. With lucid attention to the many registers of grief, the poem bears a haunting gravity and resonance, where the decisive, interior, and inexpressible supercharge meditations on time, loss, and love.

THE

WORLD

AFTER

RAIN

THE WORLD AFTER RAIN

ANNE'S POEM

CANISIA LUBRIN

McClelland & Stewart

McClelland & Stewart and colophon are registered trademarks of Penguin Random House Canada Limited.

The authorized representative in the EU for product safety and compliance is Penguin Random House Ireland, Morrison Chambers, 32 Nassau Street, Dublin D02 YH68, Ireland, https://eu-contact.penguin.ie

Library and Archives Canada Cataloguing in Publication

Title: The world after rain : Anne's Poem / Canisia Lubrin.
Names: Lubrin, Canisia, author
Identifiers: Canadiana (print) 20250118319 | Canadiana (ebook) 20250118327 |
    ISBN 9780771020063 (hardcover) | ISBN 9780771020100 (EPUB)
Subjects: LCGFT: Poetry.
Classification: LCC PS8623.U215 W67 2025 | DDC C811/.6—dc23

Cover design by Jennifer Griffiths
Cover art: Jennifer Griffiths
Typeset in Centaur MT Pro by Sean Tai
Printed in Canada

McClelland & Stewart
A division of Penguin Random House Canada
320 Front Street West, Suite 1400
Toronto, Ontario, M5V 3B6, Canada
penguinrandomhouse.ca

1 2 3 4 5   29 28 27 26 25

Penguin
Random House
McCLELLAND & STEWART

To, for, and because of
Anne Lubrin

Tout libèté fè pasaj en lanmityé-ou.

. . . you are still alive, like hydrogen, like oxygen.
—Dionne Brand

. . . and all will be right as rain, right as rain and without the thunder.
—Anthony Farley

At the end of this sentence, rain will begin.
—Derek Walcott

CONTENTS

I

WAKING
AGAIN

Alive again, under the red umbrella of the world, days
I say to endings, exhaust all the living things sideways to nothing
    such wor(l)ds to report to a dying friend, father, or brother, or water, mother,
what to know now, heaped life, coming again to this timetable of disproving
    globes, down and up under the blue umbrella of the world, singers
still singing after the rain, for dears, you-look-like-life, fibres on revived surfaces
    and all this chirping in between our easy hearts—we resemble—

first chances, the smokestrong ghost polishing love with sharp embraces,
    with cleft hands softening the burning tissue of the mouth,
gorging on exits that since our beginning would not speak of ends
    here in my embrace: until your backbones crack
the mind can teach the hand to rattle, open new jaws for counting days
    when what is left in this distance between two startling eyes
is the traffic of our watching slowing us, bluing new rooms—

    for atmospheric friends responsible to the haze, who but no one could be
here to know this hand, like mercury, is mine in this closing
    of wooden lids and lightning bolts above five indexes
of eyes preserved in acid rains, of a ghost whistling for the tea kettle

foregrounding us in this time of roads closed for walking
  the neon afternoons, the silver light, for rheumatic walking
to tanks of wastewater, to a cave of miracles where doctors say
  to me, *this accessible parking permit is temporary,*
two years must be enough, estimate a complete math
  for your someone's peculiar drowning; today, mother-ever,
rally five brimming years from the blueblack SOS held above the weeds,

  gather me, and the child you were can reappear while we are
distance seeking distance; not, as you say, while we are
  opened, keeping nothing for ourselves, not the sky at this strange depth,
not a hundred thousand others; not the seawall—part water, part blade,
  between two continents, this high above our girlhood, not yet
to our correct refuge to rum, refusing to soak your bread, not in this nest,
  your braided grass, my joke: but my groan of water tinting the reservoir,

but this fitness trembling
  at the root of all life,
but your fever for today's
  light into itself

is it time, studied, of seed-like attention to the country feeding
	each morning on the battery-powered thinker who will live longer,
even than time, feeding on the back-room villages made endlessly to bend
	from the metal hulls of cold mouths, the silver freight of your dying
trails the length of any season's tax slips, of any decade's running birth
	our dark heads clearing the egg-yolk rain; we, tumbling
we, catching us or any of our recent flares mid-bow

to anyone who comes to speak us out of air, the hot air astonished, too
	that we do not log wild plans for each other's future—
here, cleanly lies my bluest wor(l)d wishing you just any
	good unblemished year; a thousand times before a market lie
might splice us from this world of blooded hands
	all these charred feet marching away from us, we admire
anybody's guess: a *NO* endured down any street, swelled before below behind

who'd left your bowel in a knot and asked, *well, why aren't you eating*
	baffled by fear by speech by bubble bonded with bile . . .
we'll take any street now, Queen Street, Bathurst Street, Bridge Street,
	Dominica 1984, for the fevered boys c. 1914, these names, too quick
for our conjoined life, these expressions too unfortunate for any street,
	any other country, before your life nowadays bluer than earth resounds

in me it is time, yes, time's cannot so we cannot explain
　　the world, named the same as marrow beaten to glue
bones beyond cracking, circling the belly of the Earth
　　our voices for the whole of you shatter the glass windows
of unrelenting, heated houses:
　　if mother describes the world: *a*
tumour. yes—
the broad and flat elements: of
　　borders. *yes*—
like zodiacs:
　　yes—mirage of a late world,
slung from tractor factories—
　　yes—still hidden from the door,
a warbler is undone by singing today
　　yes: Signal Hill, Castries, Bagatelle,
are we forgeries until we are foregone, we—sudden and halved
　　receding into flashes at the bus stop before formalin,
before law, before order, before expertise

it is a sometimeish time for the animals,
    crossed by invisible detachment from even legs, so high up
as are the white ships blinking ahead, a head of rosettes for the hungry,
    six shrubs of seagrass, *books*, we tell ourselves,
a rock, a re-watering hole, flat officers of high ranks and mother pleading
    with a cloth bundled on her waist, who might know, know
where the world deepens its temper of salted organs, family
    shared for balance, and your hands in the midst of washing:
my mother says, *look how we are astonished*
    by the jails, I say, by the floors holding our reflections
knowing enough medicine, enough
    to call the burning world back to love

it is time harvesting hit-and-runs,
 and motherhood hardening
the ritual of doubtless love
 the time of houses unlit by grieving: *SOS*(es),
the room of my one life is full of the lights gone out
 in spite of all my protest, if I outline myself in nothing now,
a time-travelling letter to a daughter, is it that I have known
 the map, the maker of it, the doors,
the maker of them, and yet re-lettered
 near the last of time,
your trembling, so endless, your minutes dispensed at the drugstore,
 it is that I am static, stunned without a shovel
in a time of damp soil, flooded deserts, the river that recollects us

is it time again for rivers wounding down the vital pulse of undoing

    death, you arrive on a piece of paper and ancient as rice,

my gnash of water meets your woodsmoke, your oven-time

    given more honest eyes I would find more daylight

to wrest an ending from nights that do not end with nothing,

    with exits or blood thinning into air, downloading strokes

into this street, between mother's breasts, mothers (b)ending—

    entering this bare room of astonishment is my form of worship

with vowels: like *e* that divides break, ending love,

    bookend in exile, beginning end and everything,

she says *morning* to everyone, *give me your circles*, promises

    for return, spells against con doctors, against radiation,

this wind you know conducts a phrase against my childish limits

    again to survive, monosyllabic as life, my mother says *come* by heart,

and I watch someone hoard these few wisdoms

    with which, like death, I am the last to leave the room

it is time *I run, I run, I run* one day into the next into the time of games

this gameness of homes on the graveyards of origins

and this eagerness of winter might kill me in this town

even if you say to drunkards: *drive today*, and we danger north

smallened already with the silences of any Tuesday or Thursday, telescoped

days for farming, for leavening flour with our sandstone life

with cattle now grazing the roadside; fat logs for my swift melancholia

raining in my right hand and my mother's, over and over we are old as turtles

bone-pulled, pooled in a firmament-house; she takes an hour from my hand in

the middle of math class, she doubles the night soling with white light

over and over a shadow under her eyes screen intolerable words for growths

the body harbours, even bled stars, even poison, both eyes on the right,

a future, sure: all I'll remember of my face is a pendulum, a thread of light

exposed to the dark before we come aware, I am the living cost

a coming dog of war, devouring whole alphabets, from fleshly regions of the sky

in this submerged stretch, for once, even the villages are experimental
    this is no village without verdures clung to marsh
taking lessons from stillbirths, your peace-green house inherits mornings
    I meet in the mouth-formed coral measuring our singed world,
wise-bird letters to the gorgonian sea fan, come yield one hour to a skeleton
    of this world, what sulphonic grid for Haiti ranges my envy of reefs,
where must I be this flare before that poet kills the moon for goodness,
    before our walk, the length of an evening's say-so
photographed between living and barely awake, we could dance—
    the scent of our open hearts blanketing the small village
of all these singing things you bring to your lips, scuffling, now, mother,
    I am dense damp grassland

blackened time throughout the occasion of ceasefire or paper-clay

or how could I refuse peace the taste of unlovable handclapping

gyal, my mouth is a stonebox, it does trap fault, the trouble of tobacco leaves—

opening over ten days only for a waterballoon clown to smear lifeless lips

crosswise on my wrinkled eyelids three decades up so; at least, my girl, you've carried

worlds in your voice, all of them, from atrium to ventricle

without weeping for me, your starlit homologue dreamed in the later after-

noon of this hospital chart, pressed to my weak artery, working the air

black from my devotion to clay is this: these bones know usage; bones

to wait for all owning to cease, our connotations, profane as fists colliding

glass, ransacked cafés, wine is bloodening my bawl, and slow as the night we lift

our self

from day, soft against the things I will not say, like my name—a gate

swung wide out from your ribs—I demand more medicine for your footnotes you are single-toothed time, and who could make any charge

    against what the sketched hachures might withstand

nobody eats anymore; your one gold tooth leaks from a skeleton mouth on stage,

    your long fallen tété nursing, but I am no collapsed dream en zyé yo,

at the gate where yuh great world must leap into my arms, I am rapt,

    I am raw and slight, temporary like that brown map of our lives

barred on our foreheads, or the paintless mouth you wear today

    so call for this city to charge an hour into our comprises,

to charge and change no one; I leave with this voix, call of the Cabazon dinosaurs

    I know little of the (im)patience each of our affirmations embargoes

and what comes: no fiddle to offer even a slight note I alarm, notes to fill the room,

    two centuries, you know, before your verse astonishes the crowd

I am keeping time, mama, the time of stop signs and swarms
   or learning to be nevertheless transparent as a wall,
here, we've left salt at every limit, cells dividing the loyalties
   of each word we hold, abrupt in the presence of copied time,
of poisoned mandible, the open bar of embarrassing questions
   there's no ambition more skeletal than this heart leaping,
leaping like a toad in our chest, besides, I detect bargains,
   mother, and you must come again to this howling:

> *will an ounce of honey do, neighbour*
> *a piece of bread for hungry death, my dear*
> *say the minty-staleness of a Monday afternoon*, on second thought
> *what if life verves toward the heart and stops*

my too-hard skull endures for the hotness of this thinking
   the (mis)read telecasts already voiced in cause; here, not-spoiled—
we know what the living do; I am taken with you—named after a saint,
   freely into this provenance of fruit bats

following quick-time, the softening tracks cool and excellent
    huts already tremble where you walk and, in another poem,
another poet's grandfather recites a different ode, I catch
    in its lampooned phrases the black liquids of a country
of quietness draining from your throat; I don't tell you how
    this unsolvable room cleaves us, binds us again,
how we were left to your bile duct's drizzling or torrents, unnamed
    our non-weeping right eye, untrained for the marks of our four feet
along what I dread and need; you cannot have the memories I hold,
    your childhood in Anse-La-Raye, soon updated into our wet forms,
enough, we will be chorused around disorder—woman who exceeds
    how we are astonished into the last few hours of August
by the whipping work of conclusion, torso defined by a strong curve, hotly
    odoured by the interior of a lesion, a taught membrane
around our lives, the flammable-blue light of our smoked mountain fading,
    potassium carbonate sawing the infected woods, the traps
entering this story's wordless idea of a world without hail, without ill
    these are not my traps to tell

time worshipping time is a mother-image,
  protracted bone from barking spine
I reject, Anne, the ceremony of this metal
  mouth closing over your life: o-*sh-stop*, o-*sh-stop*,
o-*sh-stop*, say stop, say the passing of you from breath
  I have felt to memory I have fashioned
is this how to forget,
  I am forgetting,
the twinliness of life and death
  our movements between forms

hollow-time in this sleep-membraned interlude, I detach my selves
    from every dead doubt, what was the sum of hair growth
multiplied over each outlived year, despite resin stripping your religious
    texts of their confusions, as we might waste omens over
the shorebreak of twin oceans, footpaths, the vials of absolute trust gauzed our eyes
    but for the sake of alchemy, shrines to manman dlo,
let us talk of butterflies
    passing over New York,
meeting no resistance
    going past the galvanized sheds, as we have lately been
undertow. they are cut-outs of themselves
    at 560 miles beyond the Earth,
veining through the tall grasses unbid by our dead
    next to a fortune of mirrors and years, switched
as we are, still atmospheric, sequel of reunions

isn't it time for our phosphorescence, sounds of fur
    will eventually find me there with yellow mud,
absorbed in your remitting need, though enough and more tiffs
    pursue a paradise for you, proof of the waterlog
of companionship, the demisting riverbed, time, meanwhile is rootless
    more terrifying now
the body embattled by itself
    things we are astonished by—

it is time unspooling past time, galloping,
    lacking your speed for I, too, am dying,
mother, malachite hurdling the globe,
    16 times faster than all man-made
into the static radio of air's quiet pitch, my fingers for your scalp,
    what sounds are these, who overhears your leaving—I—
despise gravity thinning every moment since your birth . . .
    in this way had you ever disturbed
with the dirt of four continents under your fingernails
    morphing the trail of cinnamon on someone's winter drink
should I tell you not me, not she, not myself
    that in Venice I am the patient
the doctor and a fly all at once prescribing walking
    on a page ringed with your unusable floodtides,
one thousand miles washed in your anonymous,
    your tired, penmanship, grass-grown, undiminished because I beg

it is time closed to eyes in Venice: I am patient
    with a fly walking on a page
ringed with *your*
    tired penmanship, the indigo-smoke of your stone oven,
gusting, and like every previous time, time is a woman I respect
    tending the geometry of a fly, its grey fur,
head black, sand-red, solar-white, the page dark, violent, too
    round as squares; I am the one sitting
across from your memory, preparing
    the outgrowth in your stomach for its life
in an imaginary lagoon; from the dinner table
    where I am with friends, we are born early and severe,
and seagull cries record soundlessly, fugitively
    our mammalian wish to learn already
the codes of unseen cliffs, earthworms, I don't yet know
    the thing creeping in the lung
worrying the too-meagre world is
    what could stop us from running to an aid
to the lines of eight children you grew in black (s)oil
    and a bright flame lifelong overhead

these outlines cannot tire time; time is bright with unbearables
     with a tremor in your head, in the reality of your hands
is a lie you tore from the stock exchange, destined for the dreaming
     and I am a bruised and molded grammar skipping in your voice,
unmothered, how the instruments of men astonish
     a person, a 1000-lb hydrogen chamber, mother of a fuse,
why gods, she says, do not launch themselves at the moon, if zygotes,
     if 110 million mothers drench Cape Canaveral, mostly with sleep,
mostly with ink, mostly to forbid billions wasted to kill, mostly . . .
     certain blood-like reports calling back to the world;
because the roof of my worshiplessness keeps its own damning version
     of our encounters, and the poet I am, the poet lifts you
before the probe of every mouth in 2020, drowning at the coasts
     in these latter years, and we mishandle the report of a person fleeing
always fleeing, the rain falling again at this Montreal border,
     in LA, blood-lusted men with their math of horses, whip
our mothers, our vision marbling the light of a damp afternoon,
     growing light, as another poet's prediction fallows
what exits your voice for once is not the past, is nothing by herself,

it is time for rumours now, the time of watering
    our shaking heads versus fires ahead, instead, could it spread
forest to forest, is your rant against the new king—a scythe across
    continents, astonishing dead things that try to save us,
craning from our nothingness
    as we heave the deadweight
of our love up on our heads,
    how we are astonished
that the trees mature ten million
    years before our knowing what the wicked might
reject 1000 years from today
    in the face of the fragments of this life
we are drizzle to bright sky
    how, still, again we are astonished
by a single life's width, or futureless, our vacant bones' thin exhaustions,
    and for that it matters in the time of ordinary disputes
that the throat does what it does

it is time for the dark wood of undamming, the police collecting wages
 lift a hooded hand around our dread, fanning red smoke, mother,
so that bones and family grow away from ground—
 but talk to nobody about recovery, the gut swelling against the patrol,
meanwhile, to somebody beginning sleep late in life, seas still rough
 without water, without the poet who declared, only yesterday, *the sea is history*—
in a century a pontiff divides by hammering another
 poet's anti-apocalyptic report, but in your dreams, your "olive branches"
trail the sky you string to a thunderous psalm, chorus girl forever
 as the hood creep creeps, and I blare out the window: *jackboot, jump,*
and you sing *oh, mare; oh, maria,* and I think, *yes, see the sea*—
 zoning what is deserved by whose contaminated life,
never mind the mother in the middle of this story is
 startled by the fleshliness of her son (and it could only be a son)
should flesh only mean to supplant the world

it is time for questions inarticulate as mud, tell me what you see
    in your province of ink and skin
how many mothers learn the death of their children
    a lysed globe turned hot from a few hours of greed,
imagine smuggling what comes before we are astonished
    imagine a tablet made of coconut, imagine the edge
of a disastrous instrument filled with a salvific daydream
    by which world was everything sorted in year zero,
anagram of void obsession with no-death
    every dreamland invented before you, before woman, too
the bringers of water,
    the hewers of wood, denying
the evidence: two cadets swinging your sons
    on the forests' legendary branches
what do we know of your state of empty wells
    and skin flayed to paper and water and my savage ink
what worries even the species that emplots plot, births
    in whose dark fantasies we are astonished
by our desire for flesh and bones to experiment love

it is time that knows

    extinction is a winning reward, memorial to what is believed:
we can't talk of the water, the weather report, because the world must

    bend to our impaling presence, mother none of my organs,
why record anything in this myopic view: microscopic, too,

    these ugly ceremonies consume, these formulas mean hunger
in disastrous amnesia and amnesia is nobody's choice—but beauty's

    until it is, until a sharp voice waking us one Saturday
observes the hills, observes us wisdomless, signed over

    in half-burned bills of sale, the spirit drawings of the birds
trapped in the hallways of this life with infants in their bills

imagine, living things, billowy torrent-time portraits
  and what hexes volley, named for someone roughly sincere
mété nou dèwó anglais, no language to grasp the stage on which
  you can stand again, can flood with a cosmic hydrogen,
a pulled, doubled oxygen, your arm for a seditious host to stretch
  up to every witness's eye, each one's eyes underwater, too, now
again: we are astonished by your singing, *dou-dou, Kaiman,*
  sé mwèn Lanni: at a crossing, a foot that riddles a moss-heavy yard,
your pieced breeze, mother, your green scent like a big cloud
  holding all of us in theatre, in your consistent, sheltering love
what is sudden: the days thick with a misfortune, the awkward findings
  and two hacked voices sing, *girl, where you get them earrings,* wow
and your laughter piercing everything, and I am still searching for you
  in every movie, with my big-eyed grief, spiky on every screen,
pressed on every stage, into every distance, you are not anywhere, noted anywhere
  the sudden certainty of sails you are flapping forever
with a sun opening and shutting the old twang that does cover our life
  it is always you—loosed with chance against the pier,
against any crowd, any broker of rulebooks

to sing in the raintime is to work between floods

where you split: one who works and one who supposes
life demands an end to work; and I split:

one who writes and plants a tree, the reckless thanks
I charge to tradition while astonished at the breaking levees:

waking, again, at least for five hours with the birds' alarm—by now
they have spent their full song on these many days, not far

from flames slowing only on wishthink; think, then, the centuries, hiding
themselves in the open wound of gaunt men's dreams; they open and shut

like oysters before these ponderous decades, we prop away from our faces
slow time we breed and bury to enter full of see-through life

at any point, who'll ring the strange-lost animals back into our memorials,
wherever you will go with the stalled earth, your halved stomach,

the porch still light-on and barflies listening, mother

how we wake in the concrete veins of the city, astonished
    as the cockroach, we move by bafflement, slowed now to admit
we have said everything, done heaped life, kicked death between the eyes
    enter now the chickens: beat past the posts, others depending on iron
fists, broken badges, teen workers, even hidden polls, as if to say to anyone
    metaphors unmake the too-made, closing at the height of my life
as if to say to you, *I'll be literal when I'm dead*,
    I say to you this error of your clipped intestine is not what can profit
it guarantees no wine, but here now and clogging
    the streets, mother, you are as explosive as all shining animals
with four placards to bargain for more life; above us, I lift the engine of longing
    we depend on, planes drawing themselves a radius,
we swallow what recedes that new life, what hangs again,
    the future kited across whatever sky, whatever vague family trees,
our promised and seasonal flight, fighting fighting to reach
    going going going until our life is endless ours

from this long way, time's idiom, and now I turn tender with speech
    rivers idiom any short distance, mother, into your gnash of ground,
a pond, astonishing my hungry sound that gnaws and arcs its surface
    and I cannot know the speed of these noises, these fast overdoses
leaving me like planes drifting someplace else; have we been mapped
    on the last ocean breaks pressed near our nerves,
could we not forget them making a stillness of clouds, manman,
    when I am late with small things,
and you say, *look, so late you here, so late you reach*
    there, your life will disperse the white smoke of fictions some knew me by
mothers spiralled from their endurance of the world
    even if you'll never meet me in these incongruous lines
even if this poem is merely abbreviated water from a shared sky
    and you see me, a nucleus, beginning, I pretend cures or tributaries,
as if there was only reading, only the imperfect hole of my dim imprint
    on the last of my reasons milled for understanding, comparison

rest, I am barefoot now, ready for your bare hand
	for next week's sake, all talk of salesmen gone to yesterday
locked in a future greeting, promising the emissions scratched out
	of the old garden strict with dasheen and shredded sentences,
what will be sideways or down after militias end, extinction
	after extinction: we group hands according to our doings
we are young and old together at once, such bright needs, mother
	we are women omen or men or they were, and we are,
children new and waiting for the kettle to signal
	a good word to the town's cautious blood bank
bargaining our bought blood and theirs

to athletes-time, mother of twilights, crossways into pendants
    you take this wish northward to your black marrow
into the world of seas inside my mouth
    unless, for the sake of air,
your mouth opens my own
    whirring to anyone who will listen,
whoever asks the foot that it prompt
    every road given its print, irradiated motherese
vining next to such a city, over every ashpit,
    closing a wound in the abundant earth

just a tune drizzling your name in Harlem before time-folding
   nothing more, but a lesion I know now, consumed, and unsummoned
lung to grave, still you are bracketed with daylight and a spoonful
   of every animal's claw, road given my dirt, road given something else
I could not ask of your foot that it recall, Anne,
   you beside me, you who will have this place
or take your place among the blossoming reasons to forget the open air
   market in which we are rosettes of amethyst and astonished
just as we'd follow the bees in their outgoing airs and all my sisters
   waxing their crestfallen instruments along your one wet cheek
as you say, *M must be so far away now*, accepting this last note
   wobbling your pubertal harbour with all our hot days
and just as soon for the next hour we will keep what is alive.

II

TWICE
AWAKE

After six decades, a cold season; time begins motherlike
                 into the plain cold season, Anne,
a woman sways open a door, kisses a corpse, too young this time—
                 another of us in a blue-calciumed washtub
with black slime and bioluminescent anemones—jumps
                 asking, "how could anyone keep the ends
of our lives so loose . . ." a mother here listens to her:
                 daughter, dream again awake

last night and as we slept, she says, the man with the time machine
                shut out the sounds of the earth
and I was still in it sauntering from dream to dream
                isle to isle, forethought to forethought, standing
again in the middle of a road of broken flags, caught
                as if a crane would fool our eye to catch a hilltop
as if a crane is a rain impaled, what water must we breathe
                from silt following your night sweat and your will
to go sudden as the doubt of druggists, dry as the river
                you had rained in for one hundred years

you, finally, in that cook's uniform, floral-brown, trade-white
        winds mapped in the sweat of your decades; I wonder
what you know of the thousandth ring of memory
            contouring our canoed people, rumoured
people sunflowered, swinging in somebody else's cold season
            so these windflowers, are they no mystery after all

mystical, they said, since we dress our eyes with cotton
                    in the dew of our first and only lives
falling integers of rain through our days
                    one plastic bag enough to screen the windows of our lives
and only one storey to hold the future of the world
                    cut as we are into rivers flamed for milk
and astonished as shit
                    in this everything turns sour, Anne, sour, torrential
as we are from pods lodged deep in our desires

enough now, the daughter breaks innocence forever, this everytime
opens for the helianthus people carrying mountains
on their backs, rivering our echo; in this watercress living, woman, you have
gone from man to ladjablès to door, what
triumph is this when the stars are visible all day

from time's regret, regard: some words to lessen our distress
      increase our peace, a mother's loc of reptiles
swirl her into purple, there is no screen to blur the man-become-god,
      tabs cleared for the cheek turning red from black blow from blow,
but a blinking question nailed to a wall, and no one shivers for duty
      to imagine the mailbox: the message of severances
blowing, slowing, thinning,
      no faster than you, Anne,

the hour is thick, our tables full, our fields long again with cane
            some sunny day you'll offer me the laughter
of your life and I, heavy with moonwash
            moving like smoke into your door, across
that amphibious plantation, will meet you crosswise,
            Anne, with a summons: our seditious peace from the flood
from here invent a different biomass for goodness
            because I have not understood your brief,
sprouting faiths, and I should say, this is this, not that

who can hope, bright as green, for such endings
   and who could say, after this is a reward for all your waiting
if the poem must close, if hollow things must float
   if some might say, after this wilting, you must be mad to write
any poem at all, Anne,
   could your own fig tree be counted
as if a leaf, a stanza, and drown-proof as rain
   in our split genealogies debated into somebody's lost and found
come reprise these shellfire people aging in all our pages

for your dissolving island, I am resigned, repeating,

        could you know, girl, the vanishing we see

in my one motionless eye,

        my hollowed chest, doubt flooding

permanently, out of a home in pigments

        you are so skilled at this practice of saving,

Anne, and I am an animal alert

        forever to a predator long extinct

I can do nothing the same

my exact heart incubates such
        a brilliant, wrecking flame
over what's true today, what's
        the house on fire is ex-officio,
but you still answer—street gangs,
        no—switch blades, an appetite that cannot lift,
not the fire-smoke, the west all ghostly with sea foam
        not the smoke bush, defiant with surprise, the heads
of all the coloured trees, allow me to speak with me
        one moment sutured outward from this life

a notice: say Du Pan is still on a ledge shrilling

        "Saturn, god of revolutionaries devouring

your wildest children," and I've told you

        am telling you, "oh, no, you seem hostile to something

and I am not one of your lil friends . . ."

well, here, I could offer you interminable portraits

        : the man drinking his beer at the airport at 9 a.m.

        : the man drinking wine at the doctor's office at 11 a.m.

        : the baby with a drop of bounty in a water bottle

        : the woman with the headscarf on the streetcar

        where a highway meets a shopping mall, with a browning

sign: "at least give me the finger"

        I will not malign you any further

I know who is responsible in the self,

        a VIP on this borderland, on this device

this airplane mode of land belonging to no one new

: and what happens after that

Anne, see your childhood home

  we are 9 and our voice deepening toward puberty

will find self-discipline easy

   and I can do nothing to save

you, mind this burning

   resistance to still what is

wary of our delusions,

and there is a galaxy embedded in my strongbox
emptied of all sound
far from what would give
long life, to an animal refusing
that old melancholy of things
eight years before your strength can no longer hold
rain gathering, gathering into translations, Anne,
filling over the lip of my sternum   and a sigh and "well," "well," I say
for today what is past, passive, phrases leaking ceilings

this draftsmanship nobody has made, or has made to time
the horse-drawn disorder in your belly, the colonies
all hidden from our view, *Anne*

it's raw, sorry, the doctor says,
I think this won't be good news
where is possible to know, no chance to leave puzzles

in paintings, no chance
in six decades
to yield the sweetest name
back to the sorcery of you on a stage,
with the ink lines I pitch in the rapid moods of a piano,
and there is a galaxy embedded in my strongbox

there where all sound still lives

in kawenm's time, the slow faunae of my need
how to mime from my head, the river, snakes, naïve tree slopes
in the lore of your leaving, did I practise all these years for this
and of course, it is silly to mourn you, Anne,
still alive,

still alive, Anne,
and of course, it is silly to mourn you, practised
in the lore of your leaving
how to mime from my head, the river, snakes, naïve tree slopes
in kawenm's time and the faunae of our slow need

in that time-lonely office
listen with that thousandth burned ear

to the (after)life fishing skeletons out of a lagoon

to the world-beaters, mothers of turtles aware of everything,

everything returns, floats from the familiar water of first times

the bays children come to with yellow ruled paper

in these days of charcoal figures, the looming saints are all mosaic,

and time collects its harbingers
in your offering to leave me
transcribed to the species of the healed

I will give you the season of the hungry; you have not asked, *where are my (c)laws*

your tongue is waiting on its own accidental click, clacking
                    to the roof of your brave mouth, when you yawned
              this post-surgical hunger of three aching weeks

                              you knew to be brave, you knew
                                    who knew bravery

        and I will give you neither animal nor wood to eat

                    what you do not ask:

to see how I slip you into my breast pocket,

        the great anchor of one doctor's crime against three others' love in pixelated time, your surgeon regards only carbonated water

to wash his hands of this third world crumpling like a picture

of these two Plutos, proper: pre- and post-pure

planet at the synth stirring me to wash your
laurels, again and again turning to seaweed

at this last trust, all remaining prescriptions, printed, rusted

from some internet café, improvised or impromptu by the time

we reach home and I've broken again
what you believe unbreakable

and now I am not counted among the helianthus people

who leave you to enter that faithless theatre alone

little over time you have tired everything reasonable
such designs are always extreme: water pump, axle, plastic heart, chattels

                  mother grooved into life (woman horse-drawn into
motherite) I leave here all you now remind me

was always meant to unfurl like smoke, Anne,
              in the gorgon dent on your scalp
      all the unreasonable phrases

                      I hide from you
in the soft vertigo of the body falling into sleep
      I wish this anomaly in your belly

into sad-mad emojis

        I have tried to throw them aside with the good syllables
              of unreadable ends

and fast over time the taxidermy of humans and flowers:
but just for today, I'd like to be more caring, apposable

in a city bound to grin for these prehistoric risks of loss
                    give us a room far away from their reception desk
in these lasting dramas of our trace encounters

                        where are the years and the work of your hands

now, what could seal shut this accidental accord
        the coward's unknown shape with shoreline, with coldness, overheard
    useless definitions, written outcomes . . .

I lift you, Anne, where this rudiment cures time, shoulders
a need I cannot fathom
                    you who suffer always without complaint

            out of trapezing angels, out of that cloud-hung endlessness
                    you buff—no, beg in praise of sorrow,
              for any amnesty from these earth-stained, invisible helpers

to whom you'd owe all of what survives

I lift you from your igneous pacemaker

what's a direct challenge to these red lights

,   ,   ,   ,

,   ,   ,   or any other useless taxonomy

tell me you'll do, standing at the seam of a same-time, outlines for our wombs
                    our shared mouth to speak me whole as whetstone

heart-song blooding the exit

                                        exit to follow home,

        this low-slung footage of your decades,
            Anne, I know mimicry already,

                    already we are used to astonishment
        one star interpreting the other

but the black-cloaked guards who walk past your room
        supplant that future
              of poplar stencils giving you wings

        these desperate meters we string, Anne,
   at your bedside today,

          singing things hungered for, things

          no one makes of the mangled testimonies

braided to your scalp
   but which we all share, now, loosed in our maxillae

we insist you grab the upper-hand bars, in cable time

in this, yet another all-morning of things the surgeon ignored

straight-spined someday, I'll speak, Anne,
the true thing I find no language

for today

or some other foolish thing,

leaping from this asphalt time, come speak your last imago,
          or the waking harmonica
     I hear in the leaves of the fig trees, you, tending for a decade

       make the sharp rings of your furious time brace

   what for your cure, and after, what for your ending, not the better same

  what is a life in all this, visions of seven wonders out of a magnified world

but yours is a will a cure replaced, Anne and I, I would trip the wires of this life
    and here, here you are alive, dressed in cassette tape,

                                       ,

an octave faded

,

   ,   ,   ,

   ,   ,   ,   ,   ,   ,   ,

   ,   ,   ,   ,   ,   ,

gathered life, I remember no night watchman:

                  just our laughter drained into a stormed volt,

                 my wrench thrown at death

        hiding in the carcass of an old boat

     my head: a menagerie for every basin's data-pool

       I come back bearing the gift of empty hands

         and repentance, marked with godloss,

      this fumbling law of the dead

        I imagine the cocking noise of scalpels

   falling into metal cans, and your sure-fire hands cooling,

Anne, slowing all the wild herds of compromise,

                  kneading your 100-lb bags of flour

by hand, by heart, every Saturday, five a.m. until midnight

listening for the first woman with the blaring

pockets or hands of her own practiced on the hazards of silent use

conveyed with the basic mathematics of asking for miracles

when the miracle feels like theft; the years never gave

what the years never gave and never-

mind the logic, the circles it must make, I'll make of logic

whatever; I'll make of logic,

the sky and its mute thunder; I'll make the days,

as my father made the garden, the gardener

tending the vast spaces from headstone to headstone

ringing the Sunday bell, my mother

was cloud, was rain, swapping places

with the street parking, lessening new blues, time—auctioned

I remember things but not what my mother said

who said two years; who said cancer

the way death makes sense of nothing, not even

the scattered planes; I remember nothing

my mother has said, listening all night to the rain, *I see everything*:

eyes, daggers, mouths, Anne, I'm as eager as sugar in the blood

do I know when to call your priests for their token of last rites

unless you want them, Anne, and I, the living could be the last to know

a cure for the modern zeal of birth canals, commas,
and what you've been that is better, how you were drawn

from the farrow by men in vests, to a bay with seven alarm clocks

begging your bones return the DDT to their caloric laboratory
where I've left I to roost with those who still must tread theyself

I remember the story of us answering slow death and living

where the storms lay down their fret, their former
lives dragging our names
                                  through us, our unmake intoning at the bazaar
       and someone's forgetting our meeting bonds the metronome,
bonds the empty beds unmade of children,
              what a lonely stretch of night can flood,
                     what beauty, forgetting, for creatures of such high skills,

       I think of nothing my mother has said

think of us: evergreens, shaking our things,

       raising drink, raising the last *amen!* from the dead.

III
NEW WAKING

There are no more birds to watch from here, no time
      for the mountains are a hard white mast
and I, the rhythmist, incline them to home's red mouth
      remember: this is the range of twelve extinct species
remember we are among them
      and we are deux voix, together, one through one
a voice still sluicing the 8 screens of a 5-sided room,
      and here we start at the other end

together, astonished, at the islands changing debts, hands,
	les vents chaux en 1781, you tell me of
de Bouillé, holy rules that accept warfare,
	the caustic letters of Hurricane San Calixto, the levelling
of Spanish fleets, the Danes, the French who played
	the Brits at the great auctioning of ships widening
centuries, barracks, troop huts, the poor resisting
	recapture, two wooden houses left erect in Castries
to hold the dead 22,000; I do not ask, Anne, why you defend
	the future that melts the inherited brass

pauses the crewmen, countrymen at the glass dock,
      the both-sides aggressions of peace
brokered for things that don't belong
      brokered for nervous fingers to keep
how we are again what we have seen
      the years since our last revelation:
at one point to be touched by our own thoughts
      in the town with windmills stalled for years
stirred by dull phosphene as we glowed into sleep

somewhere you agree, someone ranks time to policy
      children at play even fewer'll fall enraptured by,
all the fresh orbits, the sounds of two toad choirs
      a mother and daughter is one
a mother and another and a daughter is one undone by two
      to antidote: to quickly learn one heliopause—"I count
six cities between us" and how the human world factories the cosmos
      to keep its nature—so will the small black things
explain the harbour

again, to roll up fast-fast, a perch
        something to mount through, soundless
currents, a word for this co-agitation
        no one wants to hear, | note, not even you

see now page fourteen where all bread lost its flavour
        at least, food never cares for our compliance with clearness
to savour whatever lapwing of figures makes sense today
        soifyourgod must have a taste, it must be nothing, like air

no, not stranded on contested waters, my mother's no synonym for time
        but I breach what the offing dash on Lampedusa
a dirge, bottles of brine, an axe, a collapsed boat
        her severed and clamped intestines
I did not come luckless to these unreadable appeals,
        should they know you canopy a drowning mass,
slipping from night to surface, sunlight to horseback, flood to ice:
        I do not seek this life's loud absolution
nor to moonlight with no blinkering polyps

I have never pled for this
        even a temporary recovery
from the weakness my mother wore
        the shape of a petticoat or a veil
and when I loose the salt from my life,
        come be astonished by the hives
the shape of a petticoat or a veil
        and the millionth rosary bead embossing her thumb

perhaps all the landfills will be dense always with the histories that bleed
but when she needed a bar for the nosebleed her index muscled time
    I found her a surgeon who filled her ole factory with a balloon
who filled it with water that ends bleeding on the third try
    how we were astonished by the sound of your
long godless thinning, Anne, and I am bluest again, after midnight

tomorrow is here and tomorrow again is a woman
     who yesterday was without a state but tools and breadknives
worldwide, instruments needling the pungency of brooks
     of eggs: maybe every womb is lawless, directionless, saving
blood to enter the world with such scaffolds

(it is time now, the time of red smoke
      and we're not finished yet
with our loosed tongues
      and muslin lifting from our eyes
we harmonize despite comforting myths, their echoes
      at the end of life's stemless seam
and again, we are where we were rumoured
      ironclad in our own thoughts
and the years since our last great magic—
      stir the dull phosphene that glows us into sleep
somewhere somebody agrees, we are last among
      the nations of sugared organs, where old as light our children play
and even fewer will be enraptured by the sounds
      of each leaf that vanishes while we explain
our laughter: explain and explain the hemorrhaging of our strange logics

later, a mother and daughter will surrender one-time frictions
    a mother and another and a daughter are one undone by two
before that let us meet woman or woman,
    either and neither, let us find ourselves a boat,
I'll think to surprise you with a bouquet of grasses,
    the brutal fragments you assumed held me
taut as the nights we talked the uneasy, wrecked men
    we knew, how they, like us, are astonished
mine alone could measure this

if I have been fasting for days, and you are fasting
         now, what to do with all these fires we've made
humour me, a wishbone, a flightless wing
         and upon it say, I love
you love
         you as the distance translates
an [un]openable ingress, swift gulf for my sternum
         the antidote: to quickly learn what
and how the human world forgets us, its germs)

without the soil, Anne, and the time breeding
 ardour of insects, perhaps a burning
might put us away, far from women
 eager to imagine us good servants
their threads callous around our betted hours
 and just one of us can sew a thing,
and we know too well how to perforate
 the streets still razed with every dying
and the dark knows to clean its summers
 in our bright succour at the end of the world

we burn red fruit, survive the time of a last world outdoors
      during winter, said, we feel no pain
certain fish with skin and scale are
      a quotidian grace, there, mother, ghost-swift
go with any gin for the wooden tiles and go, charge
      our last Maroon cornrowed to the family album
collapsing to her knees; nothing can scale darkness like an old life

but there is a private time, a mother beneath the literal
        where we can talk for hours about yours
gone and mine going, gone and mine
        distance is the thing you least expect will mother you

to what's left underneath, a gradual bone
     and a plover, a covey of shorebirds
September-to-September we play
     scrabbles and musical chairs until we hear,
we are sure, my compass and phosphor,
     the musical instruments in the forests,
such that forests are, unsound and bracketed by night
     press on, you say, and hand me into other hands

or do I mean my mother warned about the draft
    finding us between gossiping clapboards
the drifting brass of crushing an imaginary box
    where permanent life clogs
the escalating calendar
    our intervals pitched to the ether
and other reasons for dying to the self

suppose the silent work of flesh is flesh
      suppose the silent work of the suitcase
is the unusual work of tending the garden
      of drizzling alphabets

do not harden yet where we are astonished
in the pulse of books that grieve our lost crop
but the rheumatic heart of the blood-born
world cannot end us, my dear,
no, not yet
so here we sit, astonished

girl, did you ever dance how I dance
        if I tell you this story
where woman knew the dirge of my hair
        took me to her hip
told the bartender we were who we were
        told him *leave us* to our airsome bed
who could waste good breath on his dread solos:
        no, ladies, don't do it, it's a waste

        here is where she deepened my year, said: *come with me*
said, here's a leeway where the signs all stay
        more dark, less dramatic, so the light could fall,
fall from something not-yet-mothers, not-yet-planets
        could gather us up in chamber music,
the headlamps of our mouths

and woman was lovely, drumming fingers, beginning here again
  more elegant than planetariums all mornings
and afterthoughts, introduced me years later,
  news-brief palms cupping that same airsome
place, astonished as we were, at a deathbed
  to her laughing mother and green watchful sisters,
only one brother halved by his chemical mind
  you know well this corridor where grief is permanent,
with the great without tenacious on our shoulders
  pressing our wide ego to the sexless pages
where we impress a future tense, uninitiated for flight

I watch you wake, woman, that is all, stone and lava will transmute
        me and barbed wire into a few circles for your dreaming head
stay with me here; I have only tall answers on offer:
            let's say, *I am glad to call you here to these seconds*
            I am glad to declare a firmness to this hour
                needed yesterday
like it, I invent the rain, its ranting for a horde
        because the surf of your reckless sea crests my lungs
and my hands once ecstatic on your cheek now redact you
        to bring stories that invite any different life,

dear one, I do know more than your time-worn name,
know the mulling floors struck from holey days
　　know the darkening fear of this world,
know the river blues of blue lagoons and early wars
　　know the whetted eyes closed to this pen and its right
concern for any country too seen to face the ocean
　　the coasts hazed again, the paroxysm
of another reasoned world: the mudding city where I
　　wait for careless news from the TV.

I am not where the poet who oversees my life will go

  I am told this is another matter better left to the portraits

of a right foot, a wall on which what is lost survives

  say again that the trees and the birds will outlast us

say again that the frantic arguments of this medalled species

  are less bewildering than our charge of blooding the taste of bread

whatever, then, give whatever is left to the milestones, the timeshares

  ahead—the man who'll die of old age before he knows himself

the familial motion hooked on looking back

  at all the blackening English vowels—

how to lengthen our days, to thicken their geometry

  with hummingbird's wing, with marmite's smear, woman,

and the careening shelves of books stacked in 1906
      each with their own maddening symmetry
along a summit bridged, Anne, still with black forests; loves, then—
      astonish now, the minute hand that pulls us forward from the back pew
where, too narrow, we've been tethered to that old story
      of a mountain road, just ours, to the long day's folding
into black as though some lines with fruit in them
      rushed us into being, only in this last hour, this room is talisman,
and here I think with a black language summary of centuries
      that even where I go, I have not gone

time rusting, solid and fume, I am in want of
     something fluid in the metals of killing industry
thrusting you open, me against such strange
     depths at 8 a.m. on a Monday, new to tinnitus, Anne,
while I am prone to starving, this new-again July
     lets you address me: *l'homme révolté*, me, street-flat
with your one mouth full of screws for teeth
     soft on my neckline; I've spent this flawless privacy
in lieu of [redacted] mowing eternally our plastic lawn
     now so, who'll watch the way I disappear
now so, who'll scatter your words between borders,
     you?—water suspended between earth bridges—
you and I?—above a family drum, segue five centuries,
     heart-chronic, a beat-drop once every decade—quick as the dead

Anne, from fine-print time, disclose to the world:

    the grasses sing how we are astonished, singing, will sing forever in your wake
since it is still easy to breathe in the fog of new labours, new lovers, new bones
    astonished to agree with the vastness of evolution,
since the fiction of our lives is like that,
    astonished, the house grows fat with nondisclosure,
since our admissions break, winded on empire's playfield
    astonished, this endless house looks only mildly like our first waiting,
since the weatherwoman's best debate doubts our eavestroughs
    astonished to announce what little I've come to, you must know—your life,
since the meteorology of our windfalls shields time from the feat of its worst
    astonished, you are not the man words come to just standing by a wall
and bathing in them forever

Anne, from fine-print time, disclose to the world:
     I have first choices, sa vwé, alkaline rains I cool in the dustpan
under your house, overhead, moonwater falls from the clapboarded floor
     of your late mother's bedroom where I listened to her leave, long-distance,
and the bloodshot sky dyed itself on my retina, a study of our joint life
     primed these waters above our heads now heavier than they ever were,
more silent than a gale gone to *eternally*, eternally stalls, astonished
     at the garbage truck of our discontent already bloodletting
its omnivorous load all along our lives, since today
     our new trades with tremors and thrifted silverware,
the worldlong montages of month-old floods have come:
     cross saltwater prologues, upset larvae of bright mosquitoes, come

woman from fine-print time, disclose to the world:

    the forecast of our noontime births outdoors; how I distrust
every form of authority, chiefly my own astonishment

    this poisoned wish is why I love, I bow to deserts,
these claychildren of forests everywhere

    I love the rain, this is no secret, I love the solar wind;
hold their elliptical life in the wasteland of our third mouths

    where flowers are invisible and bones are sanded and amusing,
and every heliopause cloud senses our head, how we astonish

    our memories vining where no shade is enough,
since many who'll feed me will refuse me their names,

    and good, who knows what bargains I would make
with their meanings, more bundles of thyme . . .

    tournaments of family recipes with you at my question,

woman from fine-print time—if I disclose to the world:

    all the patrons of rank primed for astonishment . . .

you said, "all I have for you sé pwiyédyé, la vie sa la tête anba,"

    if cowardly, I said, "I need nothing else,"

if soberly, I could say, "give me your cloudburst courage,

    the water of your life sloughing on always,"

and in whose currents none drown, not me or any of my sisters,

    not me or any of my brothers, not them who eat mercy,

the inertia of a birth into blackholed time, into comforting myths,

    me, I might clear all love from the roof of this world—

since all the thoughts I have are underwater, since only

    one of them is waterlogged; I checked, I've eaten mercy,

these are all promises to the world: see page twelve,

    see page four, one hundred forty-two which does not exist yet

see it nonetheless, mother-girl, see page sixty-three, the heaviest water

    listening in on us, garbling our pronouncements all along; and you've

known all these years, what closes from any patronizing order of events

    and you must have dance naked in the rain as it thundered, in such a way

one million worshipped canticles bloomed; and you know, my man, this

    ain't no working-class gospel, but working-class laugh, yes; no working

class—netwide, zones of those frequented by ghosts, under no working-

    class moon you does appear again, emblazoned with astonishment

knife that grazes only half the garden, but check any side of the crossword
and you must have danced naked in the rain as I did when I was five
and you bawled *cut the lightning!*—these american taxpayers does sprout
a lead foot in every hemisphere; these are all promises to the world,
mild explosives, waiting one more year for every noise to darken into
the permanence of smiles, miles of poltergeists, not you again
astonished on border walls, as the breath can sometimes be inexplicable
and hot: levees do not break here anymore but every raincoat is practice
for when you leave, for crawling on rain: the thing you least expect will mother you.

The first epigraph is from Dionne Brand's *The Blue Clerk*, published by McClelland & Stewart (Toronto, 2018) and Duke University Press (Durham, 2018). My thanks to Dionne for her kind permission.

The second epigraph is from Anthony Farley's article "Perfecting Slavery," published in the *Loyola University Chicago Law Journal* (vol. 36, no. 1, 2004).

The third epigraph is an excerpt from "Archipelagoes" from "Map of the New World" from *The Fortunate Traveller* by Derek Walcott. Copyright © 1981 by Derek Walcott. Reprinted by permission of Farrar, Straus and Giroux. All Rights Reserved.

The phrase "what the living do" on page 14 will perk the ears of readers of Marie Howe.

"The sea is History" is Derek Walcott's line, echoed on page 23.

Robert Hayden's "Those Winter Sundays" figures the time-lonely office on page 50.

Insofar as the elegy can be a measure of sorrow spliced with celebration, much has been made of the rain, this ancient elegiac motif. I rain here for my mother, for us and for what is yet mine. At best, a personal façade for the world laid bare.

Small and without completeness, this poem is for my mother, Anne, considerable and acme, next to whom I am not sure to know anyone more long-suffering, more astonishing.

ACKNOWLEDGEMENTS

Thank you to my incomparable editor, Dionne Brand, again, continuously. For your light scalpel. For extraordinary and patient reading and your far-seeing intercessions.

To my publishing folks at McClelland & Stewart, superlative among peers. Thank you for all the ways you oblige poetry.

Rebecca Rocillo, Editorial Assistant
Adeeba Noor, M&S Intern
Jennifer Griffiths, Senior Designer
Kim Kandravy, Print Producer
Sean Tai, Senior Typesetter
Stephanie Sinclair, Publisher
Tonia Addison, Marketing & Publicity Director
Sarah Howland, Imprint Sales Director
Kristin Cochrane, CEO and President
Kimberlee Kemp, Senior Managing Editor
Ruta Liormonas, Publicity Manager

Boundless gratitude to my agent Samantha Haywood—Sam, you know the rest. Thank you to Eunsong Kim and the Academy of American Poets for publishing an excerpt of this work in Poem-A-Day. Thank you, Christina Sharpe, Rachel Eliza Griffiths, Torkwase Dyson.

Love to Kaydene, Kaison, Maurice. Again: Anne, if there is forever, let it be true for you.

CANISIA LUBRIN's work has been recognized with the Griffin Poetry Prize, the Windham-Campbell Prize, the OCM Bocas Prize for Caribbean Literature, and the Carol Shields Prize for Fiction. Born in St. Lucia, Lubrin now lives in Whitby, Ontario, and is the poetry editor at McClelland & Stewart.

01 14